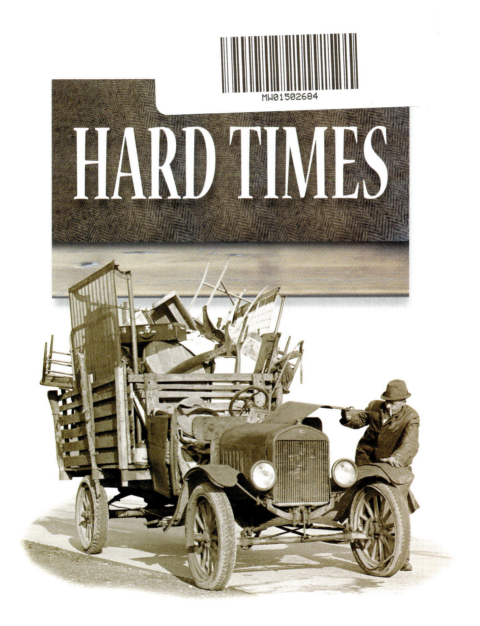

HARD TIMES

by Scott Gillam

Editorial Offices: Glenview, Illinois • Parsippany, New Jersey • New York, New York

Sales Offices: Needham, Massachusetts • Duluth, Georgia • Glenview, Illinois
Coppell, Texas • Sacramento, California • Mesa, Arizona

Times Get Tough

In the 1920s many people had invested their money in the **stock market**. The stock market is where stocks, or money invested in companies, are traded. The prices of stocks, however, sometimes rose higher than the stocks' real value. This inflation was partly caused by people borrowing money to buy the stocks. When too many people tried to make money by selling their stocks, the prices fell sharply and quickly. A stock market crash was the result. A **crash** is a sudden and severe decline in business. In this stock market crash, some people lost large amounts of money overnight. Many people, especially the poor, suffered greatly. Food, clothing, and good housing were hard to find without money.

By 1932 the rate of **unemployment** was still growing. One out of every four people did not have a job. With so many people out of work, stores closed because no one had money to spend. Many people did not have enough to eat or lived in poor housing. Nearly one out of every five farmers had to sell their farms. Many of these farmers lost their homes and moved to areas where they could find a job. A period of severe decline in an economy is called a **depression**. From October 1929 until December 1941, the United States went through a period known as the Great Depression.

Many people lost large amounts of money in the stock market crash of 1929.

During the early years of the Depression, people who lost their jobs and had no money depended on private charity for help.

Before the Depression

During the 1920s thousands of small companies were taken over by larger companies. Membership in labor unions fell sharply. By 1929 two hundred corporations controlled more than half of America's industries. An average of six hundred banks failed, or went broke, every year. By 1929, 75 percent of all families made less than $3,000 a year.

Herbert Hoover

President Herbert Hoover, who was elected in 1928, tried to reverse the stock market crash. He asked businesses to put more money into the economy. But this did not work. Between 1929 and 1932, investments in business fell by 98 percent, many banks went broke, and more people lost their jobs and homes. To make things worse, there were no government programs to provide aid. People who had lost their homes often gathered in temporary towns called "Hoovervilles."

During the Depression

In 1933, the worst year of the Depression, many Americans lost their jobs. Because they had no other sources of income, many people sold their cars or homes to raise money. Others moved in with family members. People who had lost their homes sometimes moved, looking for a job anywhere they could find them.

The Problems of the Farmer

In addition to the problems faced by many people during the Depression, farmers had more challenges. Many farms were suffering from drought. Also, many farmers had borrowed money to buy more land and farm machinery during the early 1920s to take advantage of high food prices. When the high prices fell, the farmers still had to pay interest, or additional money, on their loans. Small farmers who rented land lost business to farmers who had machines. It was cheaper for large landowners to farm all the land themselves. Thousands of people moved west, where they hoped to find work as **migrant workers**. These workers traveled from one area to another in search of work on farms.

Many farmers who lost their farms during the Depression traveled west to California in search of jobs.

The New Deal

Franklin Delano Roosevelt defeated Herbert Hoover and became President in 1933. Hoover had asked businesses to fight the Depression on their own. Roosevelt, however, believed that the government should help. With new government programs, called the New Deal, Roosevelt tried to improve the economy.

Some programs aimed at reforming, or improving banks and the stock market. The Securities and Exchange Commission is a government agency that checks to see that trading in the stock market is done in a fair manner. The Federal Deposit Insurance Corporation insures peoples' bank savings in case of any loss. Both programs were created by the New Deal and still exist today.

Among the New Deal programs that did not succeed were the Civil Works Administration, which created temporary jobs repairing the nation's roads and bridges. Another program that failed was the National Recovery Administration, which made rules for businesses to follow and included a minimum wage. The Supreme Court found that the agency took over some of Congress's powers.

Franklin Delano Roosevelt became President in 1933.

Fighting the Depression

Roosevelt's first term as President was successful. Banks reopened, more people had jobs, and more goods and services were being produced. As a result, Roosevelt was elected again in 1936. Some of Roosevelt's success came from his wife, Eleanor. She visited New Deal projects across the country, building public support for them. She took a special interest in the problems of the poor.

Roosevelt gave informal talks, called "fireside chats," over the radio to explain his programs and plans. Together, Franklin and Eleanor Roosevelt helped to bring the nation through a difficult time. Despite their efforts, however, the economy was still weak.

Roosevelt's "fireside chats" made Americans feel as if he were talking directly to them.

Roosevelt was widely criticized for supporting labor unions. Labor unions had used the sit-down strike, in which workers stay inside a factory and refuse to work in order to get higher pay. Many people also did not like Roosevelt's attempt to enlarge the Supreme Court to make it support his views. When the United States entered World War II in 1941, increased spending finally ended the twelve-year Depression.

People lined up to see the movies during the Depression.

America During the 1930s

Movies were the most popular kind of entertainment during the Depression. Many people went to the movies once a week. Movies revealed what people were thinking about as the Depression developed. Some movies reflected the stock market boom of the 1920s and the resulting crash of 1929. Musicals, however, revealed people's need to believe that better times were on the way.

Events around the world during the 1930s were not peaceful. Japan's invasion of China and Germany's attacks in Europe helped Roosevelt get congressional approval to increase the national defense. After Germany defeated France in 1940, Congress passed the draft law. As the nation got ready to fight a new enemy, the number of people without jobs decreased by half. Men were called up to serve in the armed forces. Their places in the workforce were filled for the first time by women in large numbers. The economy was growing again, but the nation was also getting ready for war.

In the late 1930s, as the United States prepared for war, many Americans got jobs building ships and airplanes.

Today's New Deal Programs

People disagree about how successful the New Deal was in fighting the Depression. But most agree that life today is very different because of changes made by the New Deal in the 1930s. Many programs that were started during the Depression are still around today. These federal programs would probably not exist if it had not been for the New Deal.

The Wilson Dam in Alabama was created by the Tennessee Valley Authority.

How the Depression Still Affects America

In addition to the New Deal programs, we still feel other effects of the Great Depression. During Roosevelt's presidency, the size and power of the government increased greatly. Once the economy began to improve, however, some businesses did not want the programs to continue. Today, people still disagree about how much power the government should have over the nation's economy.

Glossary

crash a sudden and severe decline in business

depression a period of severe decline in an economy

migrant worker a worker who travels from one place to another in search of work

stock market an organized market where stocks are bought and sold

unemployment the number of workers who are without jobs